Shapes and Colors - Formas y Colores

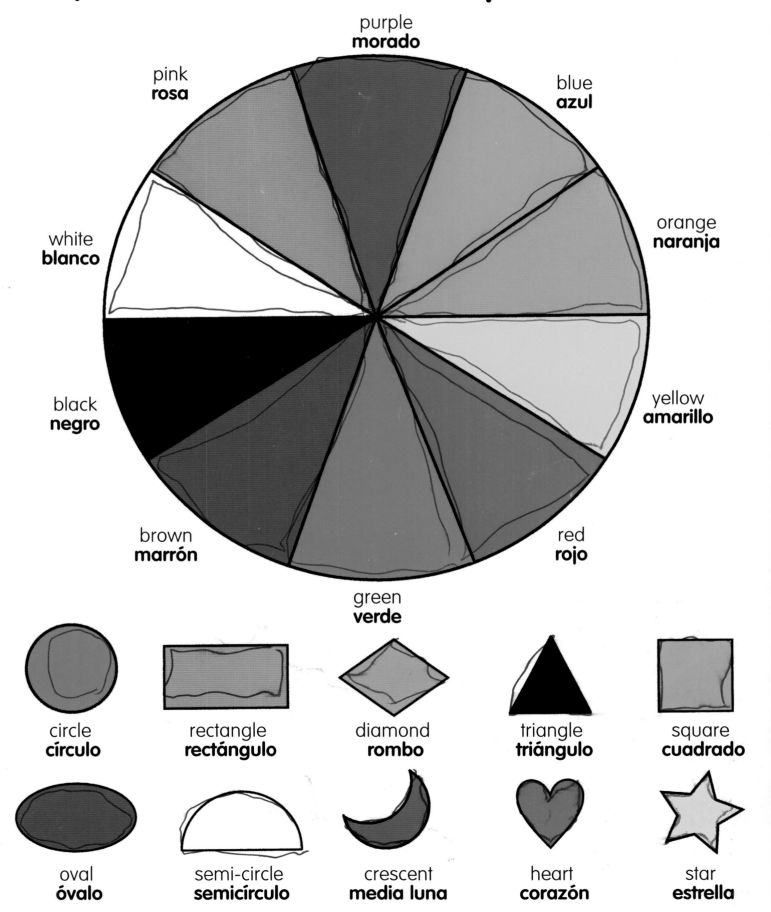

purple
morado

pink
rosa

blue
azul

white
blanco

orange
naranja

black
negro

yellow
amarillo

brown
marrón

red
rojo

green
verde

circle
círculo

rectangle
rectángulo

diamond
rombo

triangle
triángulo

square
cuadrado

oval
óvalo

semi-circle
semicírculo

crescent
media luna

heart
corazón

star
estrella

Our Bodies - Nuestros Cuerpos

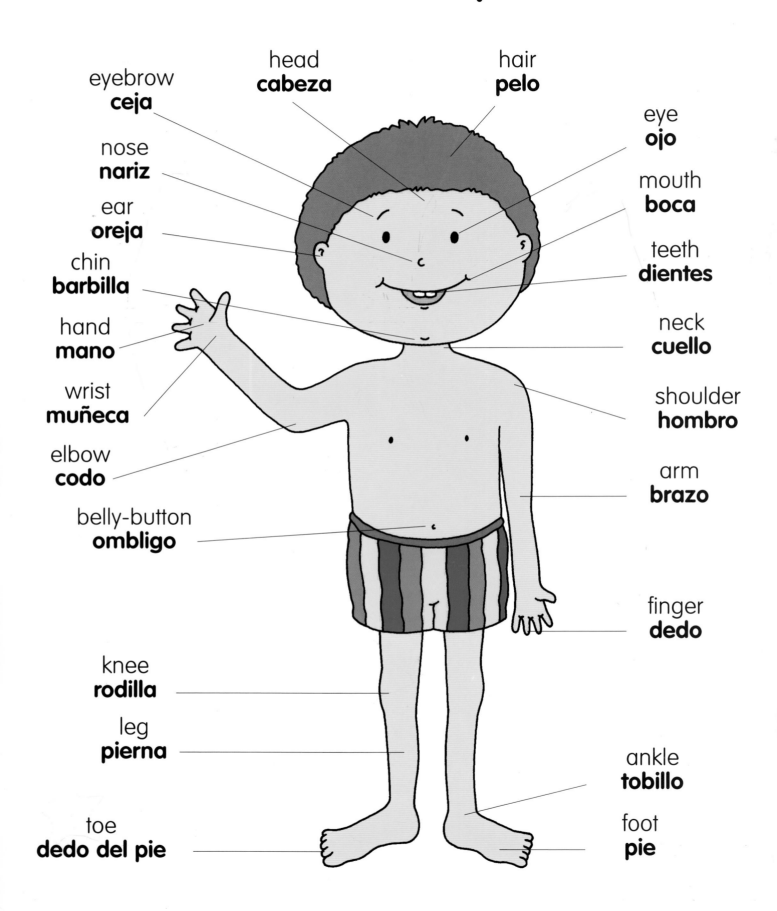

eyebrow **ceja**

head **cabeza**

hair **pelo**

eye **ojo**

mouth **boca**

nose **nariz**

ear **oreja**

teeth **dientes**

chin **barbilla**

neck **cuello**

hand **mano**

shoulder **hombro**

wrist **muñeca**

elbow **codo**

arm **brazo**

belly-button **ombligo**

finger **dedo**

knee **rodilla**

leg **pierna**

ankle **tobillo**

toe **dedo del pie**

foot **pie**

What am I Doing? - ¿Qué hago?

I climb
yo trepo

I jump
yo salto

I blow
yo soplo

I swim
yo nado

I paint
yo pinto

I sit
yo me siento

I draw
yo dibujo

I skate
yo patino

I stand
yo estoy de pie

I slide
yo me deslizo

I dig
yo cavo

I write
yo escribo

I eat
yo como

I push
yo empujo

I swing
yo me columpio

I wash myself
yo me lavo

I drink
yo bebo

I sleep
yo duermo

Wild Animals - Animales Salvajes

koala
coala

zebra
cebra

camel
camello

gorilla
gorila

kangaroo
canguro

hippopotamus
hipopótamo

crocodile
cocodrilo

monkey
mono

racoon
mapache

tiger
tigre

bear
oso

elephant
elefante

panda
oso panda

rhinoceros
rinoceronte

lion
león

snake
serpiente

iguana
iguana

polar
oso polar

giraffe
jirafa

beaver
castor

turtle
tortuga marina

Pets and Birds –
Animales domésticos y aves

hamster
hámster

tortoise
tortuga

chicken
pollo

ostrich
avestruz

peacock
pavo real

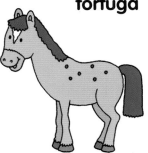

pony
pony

duck
pato

guinea pig
conejillo de Indias

dog
perro

rabbit
conejo

parrot
loro

fish
pez

penguin
pingüino

swan
cisne

mouse
ratón

canary
canario

cat
gato

pigeon
paloma

Days, Months and Seasons – Días, Meses y Estaciones

Monday
lunes

Thursday
jueves

Saturday
sábado

Tuesday
martes

Friday
viernes

Sunday
domingo

Wednesday
miércoles

Spring
primavera

Summer
verano

Winter
invierno

Autumn
otoño

January	February	March	April	May	June
enero	febrero	marzo	abril	mayo	junio
July	August	September	October	November	December
julio	agosto	septiembre	octubre	noviembre	diciembre

Opposites - Contrarios

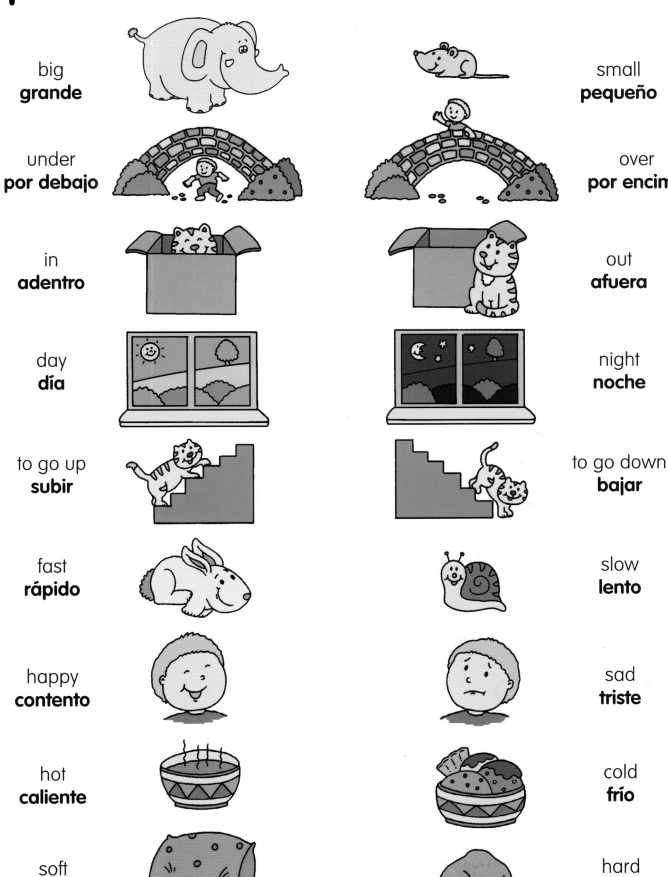

big
grande

small
pequeño

under
por debajo

over
por encima

in
adentro

out
afuera

day
día

night
noche

to go up
subir

to go down
bajar

fast
rápido

slow
lento

happy
contento

sad
triste

hot
caliente

cold
frío

soft
blando

hard
duro

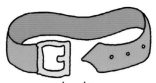

belt
cinturón

shoes
zapatos

dress
vestido

blouse
blusa

socks
medias

hat
sombrero

Getting Dressed

skirt
falda

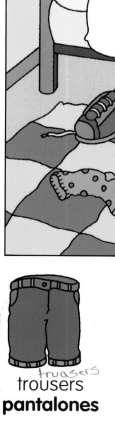

trousers
pantalones

coat
abrigo

sweater
suéter

t-shirt
camiseta

Me Visto

scarf
bufanda

ribbon
moño

hanger
percha

button
botón

shelf
estante

dungarees
overol

jacket
chaqueta

hook
gancho

shorts
shorts

chest of drawers
cómoda

zipper
zíper

Learn and Play

teacher
profesora

picture
dibujo

scissors
tijeras

pencils
lápices

glue
pegamento

blackboard
pizarra

clock
reloj

brush
pincel

paint
pintura

Aprende y Juega

apron
delantal

dinosaur
dinosaurio

chalk
tizas

watercolours
acuarelas

table
mesa

crayons
crayones

plant
planta

cloth
trapo

book
libro

paper
papel

At the Beach

flag
bandera

woman
mujer

shells
conchas

boy
niño

ship
barco

towel *taul*
toalla

sandcastles
castillos de arena

Seandcasos

Sigul

seagull
gaviota

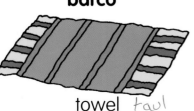

starfish
estrella de mar

ball
pelota

En la Playa

lighthouse
faro

sand
arena

man
hombre

rocks
rocas

girl
niña

hat
sombrero

sunglasses
lentes oscuros

crab
cangrejo

bucket
cubeta

sea
mar

seaweed
algas

ice cream
helado

Shopping

bread
pan

cucumbers
pepinos

eggs
huevos

cheese
queso

milk
leche

potatoes
papas

grapes
uvas

newspaper
periódico

oranges
naranjas

meat
carne

apples
manzanas

Haciendo las Compras

check-out
caja

sausages
sasech sareches pr
salchichas

pears
peras

basket
canasta

purse
monedero

money
dinero

flowers
flores

bag
bolsa

carrots
zanahorias

tomatoes
tomates

chocolate
chocolate

bananas
plátanos

In the Garden

sprinkler
aspersor

rose
rosa

watering can
regadera

ant
hormiga

tree
árbol

cabbage
repollo

flower pot
maceta

lawnmower
cortadora de césped

lawn
césped

cat
gato

En el jardín

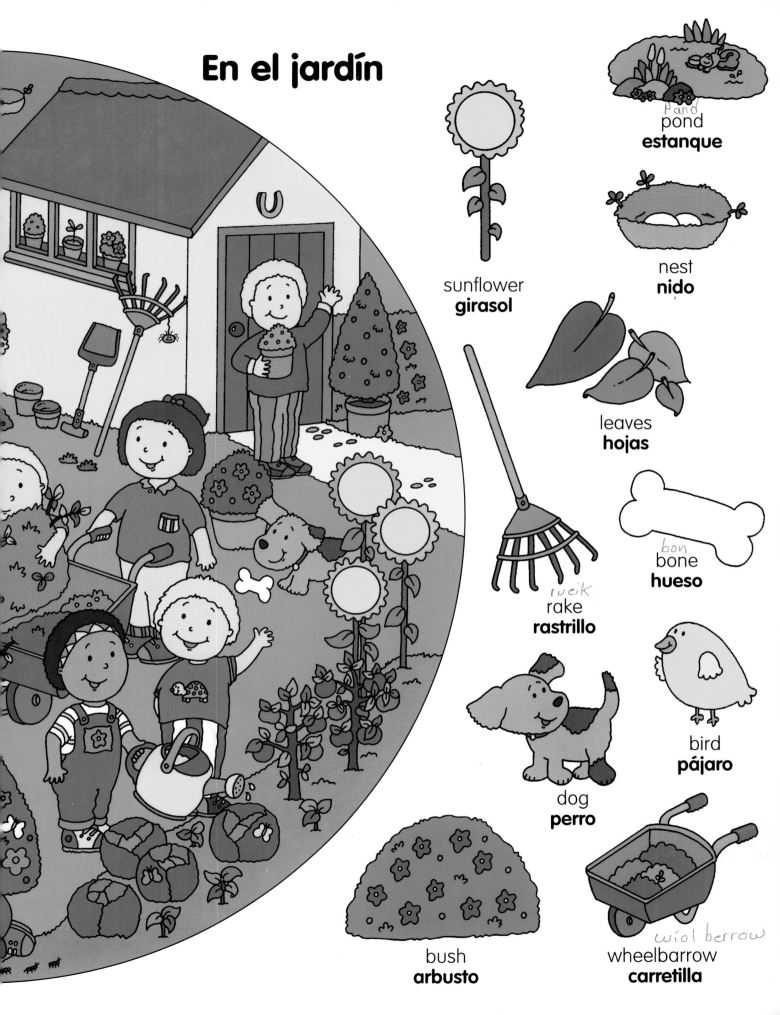

sunflower
girasol

pond
estanque

nest
nido

leaves
hojas

bone
hueso

rake
rastrillo

dog
perro

bird
pájaro

bush
arbusto

wheelbarrow
carretilla

At the Toy Store

jack-in-the-box
caja de sorpresas

doll
muñeca

teddy bear
oso de peluche

train
tren

jigsaw puzzle
rompecabezas

plane
avión

car
coche

drum
tambor

computer
computadora

blocks
bloques

En la Juguetería

fort
fuerte

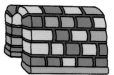
tunnel
túnel

truck
camión

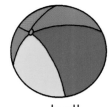
ball
pelota

yo yo
yo-yo

track
vía de tren

clown
payaso

trumpet
trompeta

helicopter
helicóptero

rocking horse
caballo de balancín

A Rainy Day

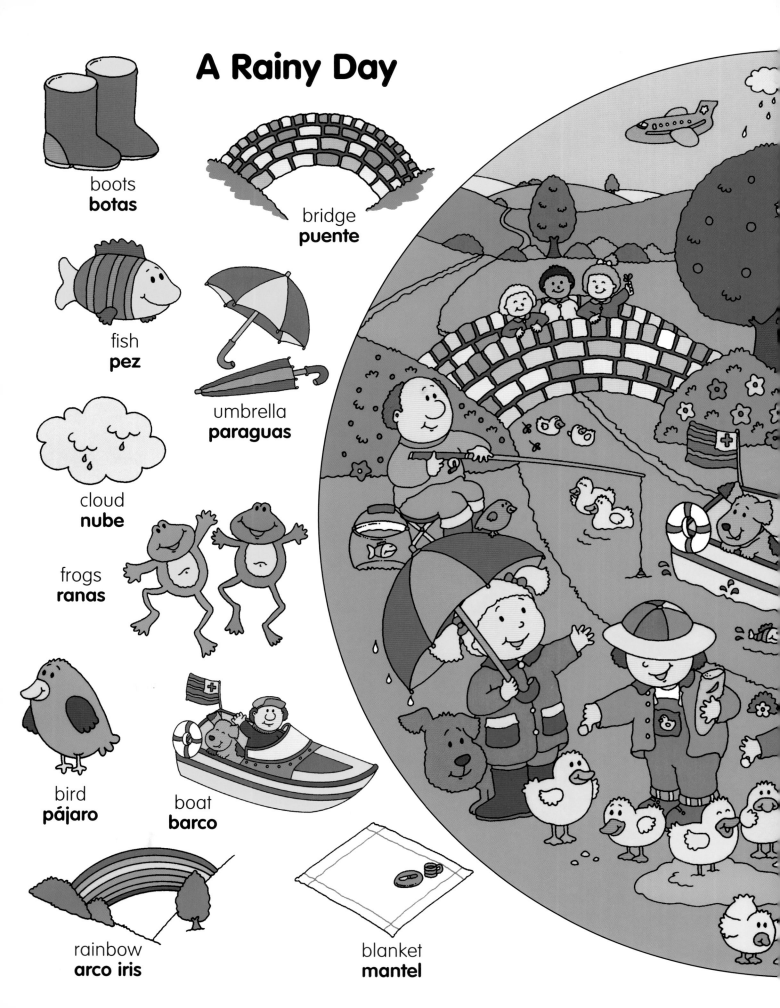

boots
botas

bridge
puente

fish
pez

umbrella
paraguas

cloud
nube

frogs
ranas

bird
pájaro

boat
barco

rainbow
arco iris

blanket
mantel

Un día de lluvia

fence
cerco

wall
pared

train
tren

plane
avión

saucepan
olla

puddle
charco

rain hat
gorro

tent
carpa

rain coat
impermeable

On the Farm

scarecrow
espantapájaros

pig
cerdo

tractor
tractor

goat
cabra

cobweb
telaraña

chicks
pollitos

duck
pato

horse
caballo

lamb
cordero

feathers
plumas

En el Parque

buggy
carreola

scooter
patin del Diablo

slide
tobogán

bicycle
bicicleta

skates
patines

ball
pelota

bat
bate

sandbox
cajón de arena

In the Kitchen

stove
cocina

flour
harina

butter
mantequilla

mixing bowl
recipiente

chopping board
tabla de picar

dishwasher
lavavajillas

rolling pin
rodillo

cup
taza

apron
delantal

wooden spoon
**cuchara
de madera**

En la granja

cow
vaca

bucket
cubeta

stable
caballeriza

turkey
pavo

goose *gus*
oca

saddle *saro*
montura

pig sty
pocilga

barn
granero

farmer
granjero

dog
perro

pond
estanque

Playing in the snow

ice skates
patines

skis
esquís

hat
gorro

snowman
muñeco de nieve

mittens
mitones

bird
pájaro

icicle
carámbano

jacket
chaqueta

snowballs
bolas de nieve

iceberg
iceberg

Jugando en la Nieve

gloves
guantes

coat
abrigo

scarf
bufanda

igloo
iglú

mountains
montañas

snowflakes
copos de nieve

Eskimo
esquimal

toboggon
trineo

trees
árboles

On the Riverbank

fish
pez

rabbit
conejo

bees
abejas

tadpole
renacuajos

jar
tarro

frogs
ranas

fishing pole
caña de pescar

net
red

butterflies
mariposas

A la Orilla del Río

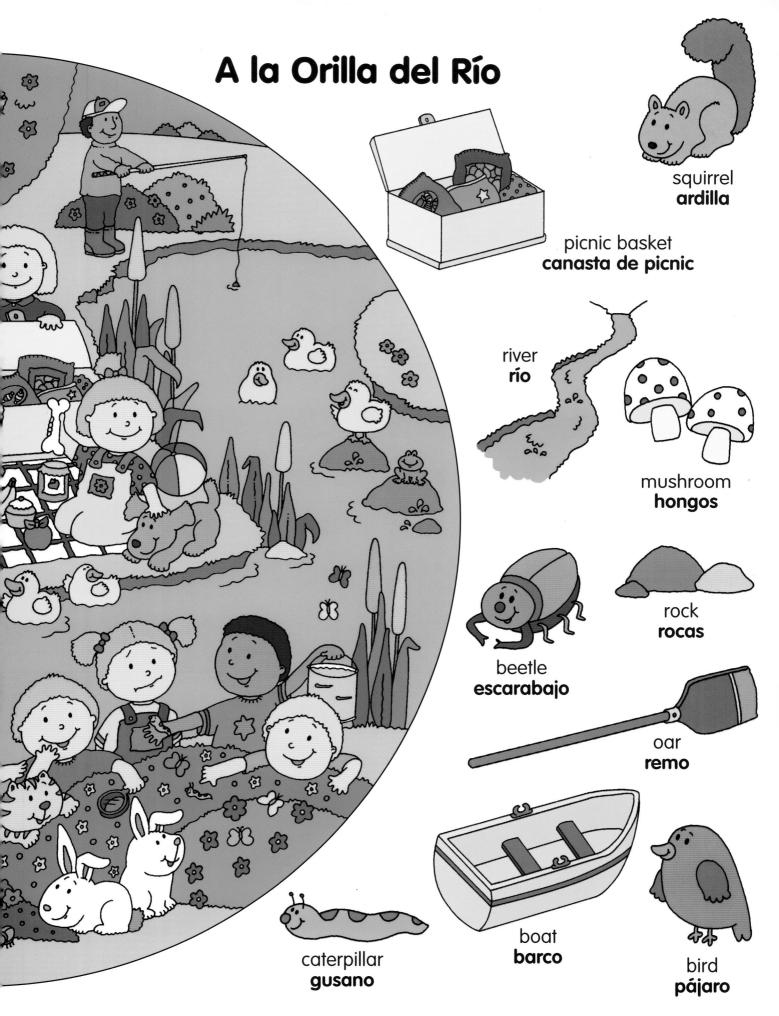

squirrel
ardilla

picnic basket
canasta de picnic

river
río

mushroom
hongos

beetle
escarabajo

rock
rocas

oar
remo

boat
barco

bird
pájaro

caterpillar
gusano

kite
papalote

In the Park

fountain
fuente

boat
barco

swing
columpio

see-saw
resbaladilla

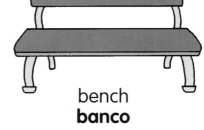

bench
banco

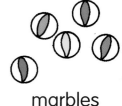

marbles
canicas

En la Cocina

chair
silla

microwave
microondas

sink
fregadero

glass
vaso

fork
tenedor

spoon
cuchara

knife
cuchillo

toaster
tostadora

table
mesa

plate
plato

The Birthday Party

cake **pastel**

sandwiches **emparedados**

balloon **globo**

cookies **galletas**

presents **regalos**

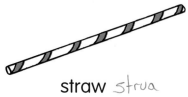

straw *strua*
popote

ice cream **helado**

party hats **gorros de fiesta**

La Fiesta de Cumpleaños

milk
leche

necklace
collar

cards
tarjetas

candle
vela

popcorn
esquites

tablecloth
mantel

camera
máquina fotográfica

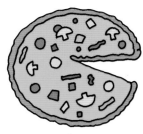

pizza
pizza

Time for Bed

stars
estrellas

mirror
espejo

brush
cepillo

comb
peine

bath
bañera

sponge *spanch*
esponja

soap
jabón

owl
búho

towel
toalla

toothbrush
cepillo de dientes

toothpaste
pasta de dientes

Hora de ir a Dormir

picture
retrato

toys
juguetes

pillow
almohada

bed
cama

sheet
sábana

lamp
lámpara

storybook
libro de cuentos

teddy bear
oso de peluche

shoes
pantuflas

rug
alfombra

Dictionary = Diccionario

Counting to twenty
one = **uno**
two = **dos**
three = **tres**
four = **cuatro**
five = **cinco**
six = **seis**

seven = **siete**
eight = **ocho**
nine = **nueve**
ten = **diez**
eleven = **once**
twelve = **doce**
thirteen = **trece**

fourteen = **catorce**
fifteen = **quince**
sixteen = **dieciséis**
seventeen = **dieciseite**
eighteen = **dieciocho**
nineteen = **diecinueve**
twenty = **veinte**

Shapes and Colors
blue = **azul**
orange = **naranja**
yellow = **amarillo**
red = **rojo**
green = **verde**
brown = **marrón**

black = **negro**
white = **blanco**
pink = **rosa**
purple = **morado**
circle = **círculo**
rectangle = **rectángulo**
diamond = **rombo**

triangle = **triángulo**
square = **cuadrado**
oval = **óvalo**
semi-circle = **semicírculo**
crescent = **media luna**
heart = **corazón**
star = **estrella**

Our Bodies
chin = **barbilla**
mouth = **boca**
arm = **brazo**
head = **cabeza**
eyebrow = **ceja**
elbow = **codo**
neck = **cuello**

finger = **dedo**
toe = **dedo del pie**
teeth = **dientes**
shoulder = **hombro**
hand = **mano**
wrist = **muñeca**
nose = **nariz**
eye = **ojo**

belly-button = **ombligo**
ear = **oreja**
hair = **pelo**
foot = **pie**
leg = **pierna**
knee = **rodilla**
ankle = **tobillo**

What am I Doing?
I climb = **yo trepo**
I jump = **yo salto**
I blow = **yo soplo**
I swim = **yo nado**
I paint = **yo pinto**
I sit = **yo me siento**

I draw = **yo dibujo**
I skate = **yo patino**
I stand = **yo estoy de pie**
I slide = **yo me deslizo**
I dig = **yo cavo**
I write = **yo escribo**
I eat = **yo como**

I push = **yo empujo**
I swing = **yo me columpio**
I wash myself = **yo me lavo**
I drink = **yo bebo**
I sleep = **yo duermo**

Wild Animals
camel = **camello**
beaver = **castor**
zebra = **cebra**

koala = **coala**
crocodile = **cocodrilo**
elephant = **elefante**
gorilla = **gorila**
hippopotamus = **hipopótamo**
iguana = **iguana**
giraffe = **jirafa**
kangaroo = **canguro**
lion = **león**

racoon = **mapache**
monkey = **mono**
bear = **oso**
polar = **oso polar**
panda = **oso panda**
rhinoceros = **rinoceronte**
snake = **serpiente**
tiger = **tigre**
turtle = **tortuga marina**

Pets and Birds

ostrich = **avestruz**
canary = **canario**
swan = **cisne**
guinea pig = **conejillo de Indias**
rabbit = **conejo**
cat = **gato**
hamster = **hámster**

pony = **pony**
parrot = **loro**
pigeon = **paloma**
duck = **pato**
peacock = **pavo real**
penguin = **pingüino**
dog = **perro**
fish = **pez**

chicken = **pollo**
mouse = **ratón**
tortoise = **tortuga**

Days, Months and Seasons

Monday = **lunes**
Tuesday = **martes**
Wednesday = **miércoles**
Thursday = **jueves**
Friday = **viernes**
Saturday = **sábado**
Sunday = **domingo**

Spring = **primavera**
Summer = **verano**
Autumn = **otoño**
Winter = **invierno**
January = **enero**
February = **febrero**
March = **marzo**
April = **abril**

May = **mayo**
June = **junio**
July = **julio**
August = **agosto**
September = **septiembre**
October = **octubre**
November = **noviembre**
December = **diciembre**

Opposites

big = **grande**
under = **por debajo**
in = **adentro**
day = **día**
to go up = **subir**
fast = **rápido**
happy = **contento**
hot = **caliente**
soft = **blando**

small = **pequeño**
over = **por encima**
out = **afuera**
night = **noche**
to go down = **bajar**
slow = **lento**
sad = **triste**
cold = **frio**
hard = **duro**

Getting Dressed

coat = **abrigo**
blouse = **blusa**
button = **botón**
scarf = **bufanda**
socks = **medias**
t-shirt = **camiseta**
jacket = **chaqueta**

belt = **cinturón**
hook = **gancho**
chest of drawers = **cómoda**
zipper = **zíper**
shelf = **estante**
skirt = **falda**
sweater = **suéter**
ribbon = **mõno**

dungarees = **overol**
trousers = **pantalones**
shorts = **shorts**
hanger = **percha**
hat = **sombrero**
dress = **vestido**
shoes = **zapatos**

Learn and Play

watercolours = **acuarelas**
crayons = **crayones**
apron = **delantal**
picture = **dibujo**
dinosaur = **dinosaurio**
pencils = **lápices**

book = **libro**
table = **mesa**
paper = **papel**
glue = **pegamento**
brush = **pincel**
paint = **pintura**
blackboard = **pizarra**

plant = **planta**
teacher = **profesora**
clock = **reloj**
scissors = **tijeras**
chalk = **tizas**
cloth = **trapo**

At the Beach

seaweed = **algas**
sand = **arena**
flag = **bandera**
ship = **barco**
crab = **cangrejo**
sandcastles = **castillos de arena**
shells = **conchas**

bucket = **cubeta**
starfish = **estrella de mar**
lighthouse = **faro**
seagull = **gaviota**
sunglasses = **lentes oscuros**
ice cream = **helado**
man = **hombre**
sea = **mar**

woman = **mujer**
girl = **niña**
boy = **niño**
ball = **pelota**
rocks = **rocas**
hat = **sombrero**
towel = **toalla**

Shopping

bag = **bolsa**
check-out = **caja**
meat = **carne**
basket = **canasta**
chocolate = **chocolate**
money = **dinero**
flowers = **flores**

eggs = **huevos**
milk = **leche**
apples = **manzanas**
purse = **monedero**
oranges = **naranjas**
bread = **pan**
potatoes = **papas**
cucumbers = **pepinos**

pears = **peras**
newspaper = **periódico**
bananas = **plátanos**
cheese = **queso**
sausages = **salchichas**
tomatoes = **tomates**
grapes = **uvas**
carrots = **zanahorias**

In the Garden

tree = **árbol**
bush = **arbusto**
wheelbarrow = **carretilla**
lawn = **césped**
cabbage = **repollo**
lawnmower = **cortadora de cespéd**
pond = **estanque**
cat = **gato**
sunflower = **girasol**

leaves = **hojas**
ant = **hormiga**
bone = **hueso**
flower pot = **maceta**
nest = **nido**
bird = **pájaro**
dog = **perro**
rake = **rastrillo**
watering can = **regadera**
sprinkler = **aspersor**
rose = **rosa**

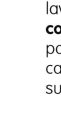

At the Toy Store
plane = **avión**
blocks = **bloques**
rocking horse = **caballo de balancín**
jack-in-the-box = **caja de sorpresas**
truck = **camión**

car = **coche**
fort = **fuerte**
helicopter = **helicóptero**
doll = **muñeca**
computer = **computadora**
teddy bear = **oso de peluche**
clown = **payaso**
ball = **pelota**

jigsaw puzzle = **rompecabezas**
drum = **tambor**
train = **tren**
trumpet = **trompeta**
tunnel = **túnel**
track = **vía de tren**
yo yo = **yo-yo**

A Rainy Day
rainbow = **arco iris**
plane = **avión**
boat = **barco**
boots = **botas**
puddle = **charco**
rain hat = **gorro**

rain coat = **impermeable**
blanket = **mantel**
cloud = **nube**
saucepan = **olla**
bird = **pájaro**
umbrella = **paraguas**
wall = **pared**

fish = **pez**
bridge = **puente**
frogs = **ranas**
tent = **carpa**
train = **tren**
fence = **cerco**

On the Farm
horse = **caballo**
goat = **cabra**
pig = **cerdo**
lamb = **cordero**
stable = **caballeriza**
bucket = **cubeta**
scarecrow = **espantapájaros**

pond = **estanque**
barn = **granero**
farmer = **granjero**
goose = **oca**
duck = **pato**
turkey = **pavo**
dog = **perro**
feathers = **plumas**

pig sty = **pocilga**
chicks = **pollitos**
saddle = **montura**
cobweb = **telaraña**
tractor = **tractor**
cow = **vaca**

Playing in the Snow
coat = **abrigo**
trees = **árboles**
snowballs = **bolas de nieve**
scarf = **bufanda**
icicle = **carámbano**
jacket = **chaqueta**
snowflakes = **copos de nieve**
skis = **esquís**
Eskimo = **esquimal**

hat = **gorro**
gloves = **guantes**
iceberg = **iceberg**
igloo = **iglú**
mountains = **montañas**
snowman = **muñeco de nieve**
bird = **pájaro**
ice skates = **patines**
mittens = **mitones**
toboggon = **trineo**

On the Riverbank
bees = **abejas**
squirrel = **ardilla**
boat = **barco**
fishing pole = **caña de pescar**
picnic basket =**canasta de picnic**

rabbit = **conejo**
beetle = **escarabajo**
caterpillar = **gusano**
butterfly = **mariposa**
bird = **pájaro**
fish = **pez**
frogs = **ranas**

net = **red**
oar = **remo**
tadpole = **renacuajos**
river = **río**
rock = **roca**
mushroom = **hongos**
jar = **tarro**

In the Park
see-saw = **resbaladilla**
bench = **banco**
boat = **barco**
bicycle = **bicicleta**
sandbox = **cajón de arena**
marbles = **canicas**
swing = **columpio**

kite = **papalote**
fountain = **fuente**
bat = **bate**
skates = **patines**
scooter = **patín del Diablo**
ball = **pelota**
buggy = **carreola**
slide = **tobogán**

In the Kitchen
stove = **cocina**
spoon = **cuchara**
wooden spoon = **cuchara de madera**
knife = **cuchillo**
mixing bowl = **recipiente**
apron = **delantal**

sink = **fregadero**
flour = **harina**
dishwasher = **lavavajillas**
butter = **mantequilla**
table = **mesa**
microwave = **microondas**
plate = **plato**
chair = **silla**

chopping board = **tabla de picar**
toaster = **tostadora**
cup = **taza**
fork = **tenedor**
rolling pin = **rodillo**
glass = **vaso**

The Birthday Party
sandwiches = **emparedados**
necklace = **collar**
cookies = **galletas**
balloon = **globo**
party hat = **gorro de fiesta**
ice cream = **helado**

milk = **leche**
tablecloth = **mantel**
camera = **máquina fotográfica**
straw = **popote**
popcorn = **esquites**
cake = **pastel**
pizza = **pizza**

presents = **regalos**
cards = **tarjetas**
candle = **vela**

Time for Bed
rug = **alfombra**
pillow = **almohada**
bath = **bañera**
owl = **búho**
bed = **cama**
brush = **cepillo**
toothbrush = **cepillo de dientes**

mirror = **espejo**
sponge = **esponja**
stars = **estrellas**
soap = **jabón**
toys = **juguetes**
lamp = **lámpara**
storybook = **libro de cuentos**
teddy bear = **oso de peluche**

toothpaste = **pasta de dientes**
comb = **peine**
picture = **retrato**
sheet = **sábana**
towel = **toalla**
shoes = **pantuflas**